W9-BZW-858

Scorpion

VS.

Tarantula

Isabel Thomas

capstone

Heinemann Read and Learn are published by Heinemann,
1710 Roe Crest Drive, North Mankato, Minnesota 56003
www.mycapstone.com

Library of Congress Cataloging-in-Publication data is available on the Library of Congress website.

ISBN 978-1-4846-4070-8 (library binding)
ISBN 978-1-4846-4074-6 (paperback)
ISBN 978-1-4846-4078-4 (ebook)

Edited by Penny McLoughlin
Designed by Steve Mead
Picture research by Svetlana Zhurkin
Production by Katy LaVigne
Originated by Capstone Global Library Limited
Printed and bound in China

Acknowledgements
We would like to thank the following for permission to reproduce photographs: Dreamstime: Dmitrijs Mihejevs, cover (right); Getty Images: James H Robinson, 13, 17, 22 (top left), Tom McHugh, 11; iStockphoto: Kwanchai6632, 10; Minden Pictures: David Shale, 14, Stephen Dalton, 18; Shutterstock: amyai, 6, AppStock, 7, Audrey Snider-Bell, back cover (right), 5, 20, B & T Media Group, 19, efendy, back cover (left), 8, 22 (middle left), fivespots, 7 (tarantula silhouette), 22 (top right), frank60, 21, 22 (bottom left), GTS Productions, 12, just_yulianna, 4 (wood chips), Milan Vachal, 22 (bottom right), nale (man silhouette), 6, 7, ottmaasikas, 15, Pairoj Sroyngern, 6 (scorpion silhouette), pashabo (texture), cover and throughout, Popumon, 16, 22 (middle right), Ryan M. Bolton, 9, UpPiJ, cover (sand), wisawa222, 4 (scorpion), yod67, cover (left)

Every effort has been made to contact copyright holders of material reproduced in this book. Any omissions will be rectified in subsequent printings if notice is given to the publisher.

Some words are shown in bold, **like this**.
You can find them in the glossary on page 22.

Printed and bound in China
004636

Table of Contents

Meet the Animals

What has **pincers** and a sharp tail?

It's the Emperor scorpion.

What has eight legs and a hairy body?

It's the
**Goliath
tarantula**.

Would a scorpion or a tarantula win in a fight?
Let's find out!

Size and Strength

If an Emperor scorpion sat on your arm, it would reach from your hand to your elbow. A scorpion's front legs are big to help it catch prey.

This is how big an Emperor scorpion is next to a human.

This is how big a Goliath tarantula is next to a human.

Even an Emperor scorpion is small next to a Goliath tarantula! A Goliath tarantula is big enough to drag a baby bird out of its nest.

Speed

A scorpion **scuttles** quickly when it's striking at prey or trying to escape danger. A scorpion's front legs can crush an insect easily and give bigger animals a nasty nip.

A tarantula usually moves very slowly.
But it bursts into a run when chasing prey.
A tarantula doesn't need to spin webs.
It uses its strength to pounce on prey.

Defense

If there is nowhere to hide, a scorpion will stay as still as possible. Some fall into a deep sleep, as if they have been frightened to death.

A tarantula has hard skin. To let its body grow, a tarantula wriggles out of its old skin. Its body is soft and weak afterwards until the new skin hardens.

Survival Skills

A scorpion is an incredible survivor. It can live without eating for a year. It can even be frozen in ice and walk away unhurt after!

A tarantula likes to catch one meal every week in summer. Food is harder to catch in winter, so many tarantulas sleep through the winter in **burrows**.

Super Senses

A scorpion has bad eyesight. Instead, its legs and **pincers** are covered in many small hairs. A scorpion uses these to sense movement.

A tarantula's body is designed to blend in. This lets it hide from enemies. A tarantula the color of tree bark can sit on a tree without being spotted by hungry birds.

Deadly Weapons

A scorpion's **sting** contains some of the strongest **venom** in the world. A scorpion grips prey in its large **pincers** while it jabs its sting into the **victim's** body.

sting

fang

A tarantula has two huge fangs. These are strong enough to bite through human skin. Before an insect can attack with a sting or pincers, a tarantula tries to bite it.

Fighting Skills

With its **pincers** up and its **sting** pointed at the enemy, a scorpion will look terrifying. The **venom** in its tail can either kill an enemy or freeze it in its tracks.

A tarantula lifts its front legs up and shows its fangs to warn it is about to attack. It rubs its hairy legs together. This makes a loud hissing noise to frighten the enemy.

Who Wins?

What would happen if a scorpion faced off against a tarantula?

The tarantula would raise its front legs and hiss. The scorpion would flash its giant **pincers**.

But who would win?

	Scorpion	Tarantula
Size	7	10
Strength	8	6
Speed	7	7
Energy	10	9
Skin	9	9
Senses	8	8
Venom	10	7
Weapons	10	6
Fighting skills	8	10
Attack	10	8
TOTAL	**87/100**	80/100

SCORPION WINS!

Picture Glossary

burrow—animal's hole in the ground

pincer—claw that can grip tightly

scuttle—move along with lots of short, fast steps

sting—part of an animal that can prick the skin and cause pain

venom—toxic liquid passed into a victim's body through a sting

victim—someone who is harmed by a bad event

Find Out More

Books

Bredeson, Carmen. *Tarantulas Up Close* (Zoom in on Animals!). New York, NY: Enslow Elementary, 2012.

Davin, Rose. *Scorpions* (Meet Desert Animals). Mankato, MN: Capstone Press, 2017.

Pallotta, Jerry. *Tarantula vs. Scorpion* (Who Would Win?). New York, NY: Scholastic, 2016.

Internet sites

Facthound offers a safe, fun way to find Internet sites related to this book. All of the sites on Facthound have been researched by our staff.

Here's all you do:

Visit www.facthound.com

Type in this code: 9781484640708

Index